**OZ: OZMA OF OZ.** Contains material originally published in magazine form as OZMA OF OZ #1-8. First printing 2012. ISBN# 978-0-7851-4248-5. Published by MARVEL WORLDWIDE, INC., a subsidiary of MARVEL ENTERTAINMENT, LLC. OFFICE OF PUBLICATION: 135 West 50th Street, New York, NY 10020. Copyright © 2010, 2011 and 2012 Marvel Characters, Inc. All rights reserved. $19.99 per copy in the U.S. and $21.99 in Canada (GST #R127032852); Canadian Agreement #40668537. All characters featured in this issue and the distinctive names and likenesses thereof, and all related indicia are trademarks of Marvel Characters, Inc. No similarity between any of the names, characters, persons, and/or institutions in this magazine with those of any living or dead person or institution is intended, and any such similarity which may exist is purely coincidental. **Printed in the U.S.A.** ALAN FINE, EVP - Office of the President, Marvel Worldwide, Inc. and EVP & CMO Marvel Characters B.V.; DAN BUCKLEY, Publisher & President - Print, Animation & Digital Divisions; JOE QUESADA, Chief Creative Officer; TOM BREVOORT, SVP of Publishing; DAVID BOGART, SVP of Operations & Procurement, Publishing; RUWAN JAYATILLEKE, SVP & Associate Publisher, Publishing; C.B. CEBULSKI, SVP of Creator & Content Development; DAVID GABRIEL, SVP of Publishing Sales & Circulation; MICHAEL PASCIULLO, SVP of Brand Planning & Communications; JIM O'KEEFE, VP of Operations & Logistics; DAN CARR, Executive Director of Publishing Technology; SUSAN CRESPI, Editorial Operations Manager; ALEX MORALES, Publishing Operations Manager; STAN LEE, Chairman Emeritus. For information regarding advertising in Marvel Comics or on Marvel.com, please contact John Dokes, SVP Integrated Sales and Marketing, at jdokes@marvel.com. For Marvel subscription inquiries, please call 800-217-9158. **Manufactured between 4/2/2012 and 4/23/2012 by SHERIDAN BOOKS, INC., CHELSEA, MI, USA.**

10 9 8 7 6 5 4 3 2 1

# OZMA OF OZ

ADAPTED FROM THE NOVEL BY L. FRANK BAUM

Writer: **ERIC SHANOWER**
Artist: **SKOTTIE YOUNG**
Colorist: **JEAN-FRANCOIS BEAULIEU**
Letterer: **JEFF ECKLEBERRY**

Production: **DAMIEN LUCCHESE, TAYLOR ESPOSITO, MAYA GUTIERREZ & MANNY MEDEROS**
Assistant Editor: **MICHAEL HORWITZ**
Editors: **SANA AMANAT & NATE COSBY**

Collection Editor: **MARK D. BEAZLEY**
Assistant Editors: **NELSON RIBEIRO & ALEX STARBUCK**
Editor, Special Projects: **JENNIFER GRÜNWALD**
Senior Editor, Special Projects: **JEFF YOUNGQUIST**
Senior Vice President of Sales: **DAVID GABRIEL**
SVP of Brand Planning & Communications: **MICHAEL PASCIULLO**
Book Design: **ARLENE SO**

Editor in Chief: **AXEL ALONSO**
Chief Creative Officer: **JOE QUESADA**
Publisher: **DAN BUCKLEY**
Executive Producer: **ALAN FINE**

# DOROTHY GALE IS BACK

The main character of author L. Frank Baum's best-selling 1900 children's book, *The Wonderful Wizard of Oz*, was a Kansas farm girl named Dorothy who found herself in the strange and magical Land of Oz. Her goal was to return home. Baum's 1904 sequel, *The Marvelous Land of Oz*, barely mentioned Dorothy. Instead, the returning characters from the first book were Dorothy's Oz friends, the Scarecrow and the Tin Woodman. But readers demanded "more about Dorothy."

So in the third Oz book, *Ozma of Oz*, published in 1907, Dorothy Gale returned to Oz, and the Oz books officially became a series.

In *Ozma of Oz* L. Frank Baum could have mimicked the plot of *The Wonderful Wizard of Oz* by again giving his young heroine the goal of returning home. But Baum consciously tried to make each of his Oz stories unique. *Ozma of Oz* is tightly plotted and introduces many new characters destined to become mainstays of the Oz cast. When I read it first as a child, it immediately became my favorite Oz book. I know that I'm not alone in that experience.

Dorothy's main role in the story is as an ally to her new friend, Ozma, ruler of Oz. Ozma's goal is to free a group of slaves from another country by leading her army against the ruler of a third country. Much criticism has been leveled over the years at Ozma's foreign policy, which tends to be well intentioned but naïve. What her critics seem to forget is that Ozma is new to ruling a country. Her upbringing as a witch's servant was no fit preparation for dealing with affairs of state. She's a kid suddenly saddled with adult responsibility, still feeling her way as a monarch after her surprise discovery at the end of the previous Oz book. Some of her advisors have experience as rulers—the Tin Woodman, Glinda, the Scarecrow, and the Cowardly Lion. But youthful, inexperienced Ozma must largely rely on her own judgment. Yet even in the face of danger and her own mistakes Ozma never falters, as you'll see.

*Ozma of Oz* also features the return of the Cowardly Lion. Near the end of *The Wonderful Wizard of Oz* the Lion became King of Beasts. But from now on, he evidently takes up permanent residence in the Emerald City. He mentions his forest kingdom once in this story, but after that we never hear about it again.

The Scarecrow, the Tin Woodman, and the Sawhorse are back, too. Lots of other Oz characters from the first two books make appearances: Jack Pumpkinhead, the Woggle-bug, Jinjur, Jellia Jamb, even Boq the Munchkin—see if you can spot him.

But it wouldn't be an Oz book without plenty of new characters. Viewers of the 1985 Disney motion picture *Return to Oz* will recognize several of them in cartoonist Skottie Young's captivating new designs. Foremost are Billina the Yellow Hen, who doesn't stand for any nonsense, and Tik-tok, the copper Clockwork Man, who can do anything but actually live. The vain and self-absorbed Princess Langwidere with her cabinet of detachable heads also appeared in the movie *Return to Oz*—though there she was called Mombi, possibly because the play on words "languid air" was too obscure.

And here's the first appearance of the Nome King, the arch villain of the Oz books. Initially the Nome King doesn't seem like such a bad guy. Outwardly he's reasonable, even jolly. But like any good literary villain, the Nome King has deeper layers. And some of them are anything but reasonable. Many of the Nome King's justifications for his actions are as valid as any politician's, before or since. If you'd like an exercise in critical thinking, pay attention to the Nome King's debate with Dorothy about the King of Ev's long life.

*Ozma of Oz* has been adapted many times—to motion pictures, to the stage, to animation, to picture books, to comics art. I'd like to mention two instances.

First, L. Frank Baum, as he'd done with his previous Oz books, adapted *Ozma of Oz* into a stage musical. After several incarnations, the production finally reached the stage in 1913 as *The Tik-tok Man of Oz*, with music by Louis F. Gottschalk. The show played successfully in California and toured the Midwest, but never reached Broadway. Baum recycled much of the show's plot and many of its characters into his Oz book for 1914, *Tik-tok of Oz*.

Second, there was a previous Marvel Comics adaptation of *Ozma of Oz*. In 1975 Marvel Comics and DC Comics teamed up for the first time to publish *MGM's Marvelous Wizard of Oz*. It was an oversized comic book—in the format called a Treasury Edition—adapting the 1939 MGM movie adaptation of Baum's first Oz book. The art was penciled by John Buscema, who captured a close retelling of the movie, despite having seen it only once decades before. The script was by Roy Thomas, who also wrote the script for the follow-up, *The Marvelous Land of Oz* Treasury Edition, issued the next year by Marvel Comics alone. Its lush artwork by Alfredo Alcala was based on John R. Neill's original illustrations for the book, except in the depictions of the Scarecrow and the Tin Woodman, who resembled their MGM movie versions.

An advertisement in the *Marvelous Land* Treasury Edition announced *The Marvelous Ozma of Oz*, coming later in 1976, again with art by Alcala and script by Thomas. The completed project was a faithful adaptation of Baum's book, sprinkled with a handful of characters based on their MGM movie counterparts. This adherence to the MGM movie necessitated the Hungry Tiger walking on his hind legs to match the Cowardly Lion. As scripter Roy Thomas has noted elsewhere, the result was a bit odd-looking when the two characters pulled Ozma's chariot.

Back then, as I understand it, Marvel's legal department had determined that three Oz titles were in the public domain. The first two were *The Wonderful Wizard of Oz* and *The Marvelous Land of Oz*. But the third title wasn't Baum's third Oz book, *Ozma of Oz*, as had been assumed. It was actually *The New Wizard of Oz*, merely a retitling of *The Wonderful Wizard of Oz*. When Marvel realized that *Ozma of Oz* was still under copyright, rather than secure publication rights from Baum's heirs, they simply cancelled publication.

Today there's little chance of the first Marvel Comics adaptation of *Ozma of Oz* being published. While L. Frank Baum's *Ozma of Oz* has since entered public domain, the rights to the likenesses of the MGM movie characters would need to be secured again. An even greater hurdle to publication is the state of the artwork, assuming the art could be located. Photocopies of the art show that many word balloons—originally pasted onto Alcala's artwork—have fallen off. Restoration would be a major undertaking.

One fragment of the project, however, saw print. The front cover by John Romita—with coloring by yours truly—appeared on the back cover of a 1987 issue of *The Baum Bugle*, the journal of the International Wizard of Oz Club (whose web address is www.ozclub.org for those interested).

But now Marvel Comics presents a new comics version of *Ozma of Oz* for the enjoyment of all. So what are you waiting for? Turn the page and start enjoying Dorothy Gale's return.

Eric Shanower
July 2011

IT WAS LUCKY FOR DOROTHY THAT THE STORM BEGAN TO QUIET DOWN. OTHERWISE, SHE MIGHT HAVE PERISHED.

I SUPPOSE MANY OTHERS IN MY PLACE WOULD WEEP AND GIVE WAY TO DESPAIR. BUT I'VE HAD SO MANY ADVENTURES AND COME SAFELY THROUGH THEM.

I'LL JUST HAVE TO PATIENTLY WAIT FOR WHATEVER MY FATE MIGHT BE.

I'M WET AND UNCOMFORTABLE, IT'S TRUE. BUT SLEEP WILL BE THE BEST THING TO RESTORE MY STRENGTH...

...AND THE EASIEST WAY TO PASS THE TIME.

IF WE WERE IN THE LAND OF OZ, I WOULDN'T THINK IT SO STRANGE. MANY ANIMALS CAN TALK IN THAT COUNTRY. BUT OUT HERE IN THE OCEAN MUST BE A LONG WAY FROM OZ.

HOW'S MY GRAMMAR? DO I SPEAK QUITE PROPERLY?

THE RED ROOSTER HAS OFTEN SAID THAT MY CLUCK AND CACKLE WERE QUITE PERFECT.

YOU DO VERY WELL FOR A BEGINNER.

IT'S A COMFORT TO KNOW I'M TALKING PROPERLY.

WHY, WE'RE NOT FAR FROM LAND!

WHERE? WHERE IS IT?

OVER THERE A LITTLE WAY.

WE SEEM TO BE DRIFTING TOWARD IT. BEFORE NOON WE OUGHT TO FIND OURSELVES UPON DRY LAND AGAIN.

I HOPE WE'LL FIND SOMETHING TO EAT. IT'S LONG PAST BREAKFAST TIME.

YOU MAY AS WELL EAT THIS EGG.

I COULDN'T UNLESS IT WAS COOKED.

DON'T YOU WANT TO HATCH IT?

I NEVER CARE TO HATCH EGGS UNLESS I'VE A NICE SNUG NEST IN A QUIET PLACE WITH A BAKER'S DOZEN OF EGGS UNDER ME.

THAT'S THIRTEEN, YOU KNOW--A LUCKY NUMBER FOR HENS.

PERHAPS IT WAS LOST BY SOMEBODY WHO LIVES FAR AWAY, BUT ONCE WANDERED ON THIS VERY SHORE.

I BELIEVE, BILLINA, I'LL HAVE A LOOK 'ROUND AND SEE IF I CAN FIND SOME BREAK-FAST.

SOON.

HOW ODD. LETTERS IN THE SAND... WHAT DOES IT SAY?

HOW SHOULD I KNOW? I CANNOT READ. I'VE NEVER BEEN TO SCHOOL, YOU KNOW.

WELL, I HAVE -- BUT THE LETTERS ARE SO BIG AND FAR APART, IT'S HARD TO SPELL OUT THE WORDS.

B--E--W--A--

AND THE LEAVES ARE ALL PAPER NAPKINS!

LOOK, BILLINA. *THIS* TREE IS EVEN *MORE* WONDERFUL-- IT BEARS TIN DINNER PAILS!

A LUNCH ISN'T EXACTLY BREAKFAST, BUT WHEN ONE IS HUNGRY, ONE CAN EVEN EAT SUPPER IN THE MORNING AND NOT COMPLAIN.

A HAM SANDWICH, A PIECE OF SPONGE CAKE, A PICKLE, A SLICE OF CHEESE, AND AN APPLE!

AND EACH THING HAS A SEPARATE STEM.

I HOPE YOUR LUNCH-BOX IS PERFECTLY RIPE. SO MUCH SICK-NESS IS CAUSED BY EATING GREEN THINGS.

NO, MISS. I'M HER SERVANT.

MAY I SEE THE PRINCESS, PLEASE?

I'LL ASK HER TO GRANT YOU AN AUDIENCE, MISS. STEP IN, PLEASE, AND TAKE A SEAT IN THE DRAWING-ROOM.

SHOO! SHOO!

SHOO, YOURSELF! HAVEN'T YOU ANY BETTER MANNERS THAN THAT?

OH, DO YOU TALK?

CAN'T YOU HEAR ME? DROP THAT APRON AND GET OUT OF THE DOORWAY, SO THAT I MAY ENTER WITH MY FRIENDS!

THE PRINCESS WON'T LIKE IT!

I DON'T CARE WHETHER SHE LIKES IT OR NOT!

THERE COME MY BELOVED FRIENDS FROM OZ—THE SCARECROW—THE TIN WOODMAN—THE COWARDLY LION! *I'M AS GOOD AS RESCUED!*

DO YOU THINK I'D LET THAT SPECKLED VILLAIN OF A ROOSTER LORD IT OVER *ME* AND CLAIM TO RUN THIS CHICKEN HOUSE? NOT IF MY NAME IS BILL!

IT ISN'T BILL, IT'S BILLINA.

COME HERE. OZMA OF OZ IS HERE, AND HAS SET US FREE.

OH, BILLINA! YOU'VE LOST A LOT OF FEATHERS, ONE OF YOUR EYES IS NEARLY PECKED OUT, AND YOUR COMB IS BLEEDING!

THAT'S NOTHING. JUST LOOK AT THE SPECKLED ROOSTER! DIDN'T I DO HIM UP BROWN?

I DON'T APPROVE AT ALL. AND YOU'RE TALKING SLANG, WHICH IS VERY UNDIGNIFIED. THOSE COMMON CHICKENS WOULD SOON SPOIL YOUR GOOD MANNERS.

I WAS RAISED IN THE UNITED STATES, AND I WON'T ALLOW ANY ONE-HORSE CHICKEN OF THE LAND OF EV TO RUN OVER ME AND PUT ON AIRS.

BUT I DIDN'T ASK TO ASSOCIATE WITH THEM. THAT CROSS OLD PRINCESS IS TO BLAME.

*D*OROTHY INTRODUCED THE YELLOW HEN TO THE COWARDLY LION AND THE HUNGRY TIGER.

TO JUDGE BY YOUR PRESENT APPEARANCE, YOU'RE NOT A COWARD, AS I AM.

WHY, THEY SEEM TO BE ALL OFFICERS.

THEY ARE, ALL EXCEPT ONE.

I HAVE IN MY ARMY EIGHT GENERALS, SIX COLONELS, SEVEN MAJORS AND FIVE CAPTAINS...

...BESIDES ONE PRIVATE FOR THEM TO COMMAND. I'D LIKE TO PROMOTE THE PRIVATE, FOR NO PRIVATE SHOULD EVER BE IN PUBLIC LIFE. BESIDES, OFFICERS ARE MORE IMPORTANT LOOKING, AND LEND DIGNITY TO OUR ARMY.

NO DOUBT YOU'RE RIGHT.

Why should you fight the Nome King? He has done no wrong.

NO WRONG! ISN'T IT WRONG TO IMPRISON A QUEEN MOTHER AND HER TEN CHILDREN?

They were sold to the Nome King by King Ev-ol-do. It was the King of Ev who did wrong, and when he re-al-ized what he had done he drowned him-self.

THIS IS NEWS TO ME. I'D SUPPOSED THE NOME KING WAS ALL TO BLAME. BUT IN ANY CASE, HE MUST BE MADE TO LIBERATE THE PRISONERS.

MY UNCLE EVOLDO WAS A VERY WICKED MAN. IF HE'D DROWNED HIMSELF *BEFORE* HE SOLD HIS FAMILY, NO ONE WOULD HAVE CARED.

BUT HE SOLD THEM IN EXCHANGE FOR A LONG LIFE, AND AFTERWARD, DESTROYED THE LIFE BY JUMPING INTO THE SEA.

THEN HE DID NOT GET THE LONG LIFE, AND THE NOME KING MUST GIVE UP THE PRISONERS. WHERE ARE THEY CONFINED?

THE KING, WHOSE NAME IS ROQUAT OF THE ROCKS, OWNS A SPLENDID PALACE UNDERNEATH THE GREAT MOUNTAIN AT THE NORTH END OF THIS KINGDOM.

HE'S TRANSFORMED THE QUEEN AND HER CHILDREN INTO ORNAMENTS AND BRIC-A-BRAC TO DECORATE HIS ROOMS.

I'D LIKE TO KNOW WHO THIS NOME KING IS.

THAT NIGHT DOROTHY SLEPT IN A BEDCHAMBER NEXT TO THAT OCCUPIED BY OZMA OF OZ.

BEFORE DAYBREAK EVERYONE WAS AWAKE AND STIRRING.

THE LION AND TIGER WERE HARNESSED.

AND THE PARTY STARTED FOR THE NOME KING'S PALACE.

THE GENERALS COMMANDED THE COLONELS.

THE COLONELS COMMANDED THE MAJORS.

THE MAJORS COMMANDED THE CAPTAINS.

THE CAPTAINS COMMANDED THE PRIVATE.

AND THE PRIVATE MARCHED WITH AN AIR OF PROUD IMPORTANCE BECAUSE IT REQUIRED SO MANY OFFICERS TO GIVE HIM HIS ORDERS.

MARCH! MARCH! MARCH! MARCH!

HAH HAH HAH HEE HEE...

WHAT ARE THEY?

Do not mind them. They are on-ly the Nomes--the rock fair-ies who serve the Nome King. They will do us no harm.

You must call for the King, be-cause with-out him you can ne-ver find the en-trance to the pal-ace.

HEE HEE HEEEEE...

RIGHT-ABOUT-FACE!

HALT! WHERE ARE YOU GOING?

I--I'VE FORGOTTEN THE BRUSH FOR MY WHISKERS! S-S-SO WE'RE G-GOING BACK AFTER IT!

COME WITH ME FOR A MOMENT, MY DEAR OZMA.

HEH HEH!

TRAMP TRAMP TRAMP TRAMP...

YIPE!

YOW!

IT WASN'T LONG BEFORE--

NEXT!

THUS, ONE AFTER ANOTHER, ALL OF THE TWENTY-SIX OFFICERS FILED INTO THE PALACE AND MADE THEIR GUESSES -- AND BECAME ORNAMENTS.

THE PRIVATE NEXT TOOK HIS TURN.

FAREWELL -- SNIFF!

WHILE THEY WAITED, THE NOME KING ORDERED REFRESHMENTS.

YOUR MAJESTY MUST NOT EAT TOO MUCH CAKE SO LATE AT NIGHT, OR YOU'LL BE ILL.

YOU'LL FIND THE COFFEE EXCELLENT--MADE OF A RICHLY FLAVORED CLAY, BROWNED IN THE FURNACES AND THEN GROUND FINE.

IT'S NOT AT ALL MUDDY!

YOU'VE NO BUSINESS TO SIT UP SO LATE. YOU'LL BE CROSS AS A GRIFFIN TOMORROW.

AS SOON AS THAT STUPID PRIVATE IS TRANSFORMED, KALIKO, WE'LL ALL GO TO BED AND LEAVE THE JOB TO BE FINISHED IN THE MORNING.

IS IT SO VERY LATE?

WHY, IT'S AFTER MIDNIGHT--THAT STRIKES ME AS BEING LATE ENOUGH.

THERE IS NEITHER NIGHT NOR DAY IN MY KINGDOM BECAUSE IT'S UNDER THE EARTH'S SURFACE, WHERE THE SUN DOESN'T SHINE.

BUT WE NOMES HAVE TO SLEEP, JUST THE SAME AS THE UPSTAIRS PEOPLE DO.

THERE! THE PRIVATE MADE HIS LAST GUESS. OF COURSE HE GUESSED WRONGLY, AND OF COURSE HE BECAME AN ORNAMENT.

CHIEF STEWARD, SHOW THESE GUESTS TO SOME OF THE SLEEPING APARTMENTS -- AND BE QUICK ABOUT IT, TOO, FOR I'M DREADFULLY SLEEPY MYSELF!

AH! A NICE DARK PLACE IN WHICH TO GO TO SLEEP.

ZZZ...

TAKE IT AWAY!

TAKE IT AWAY AT ONCE!

I CAN'T-- I HAVEN'T ANY HANDS.

I'LL TAKE IT. I'M MAKING A COLLECTION OF BILLINA'S EGGS. I ALREADY HAVE ONE SHE LAID YESTERDAY.

STOP! DON'T TAKE THE EGG UNLESS THE KING WILL ALLOW ME TO ENTER THE PALACE AND GUESS AS THE OTHERS HAVE DONE.

HAW! YOU'RE ONLY A HEN. HOW COULD YOU GUESS MY ENCHANTMENTS?

I CAN TRY, I SUPPOSE. ALSO, I MUST HAVE THE RIGHT TO GUESS THE ENCHANTMENTS OF MY FRIENDS. AND IF I FAIL, YOU'LL HAVE ANOTHER ORNAMENT.

A PRETTY ORNAMENT YOU'D MAKE, WOULDN'T YOU? VERY WELL, YOU SHALL HAVE YOUR WAY. YOU HAVE MY PROMISE.

IT WILL PROPERLY PUNISH YOU FOR DARING TO LAY AN EGG IN MY PRESENCE!

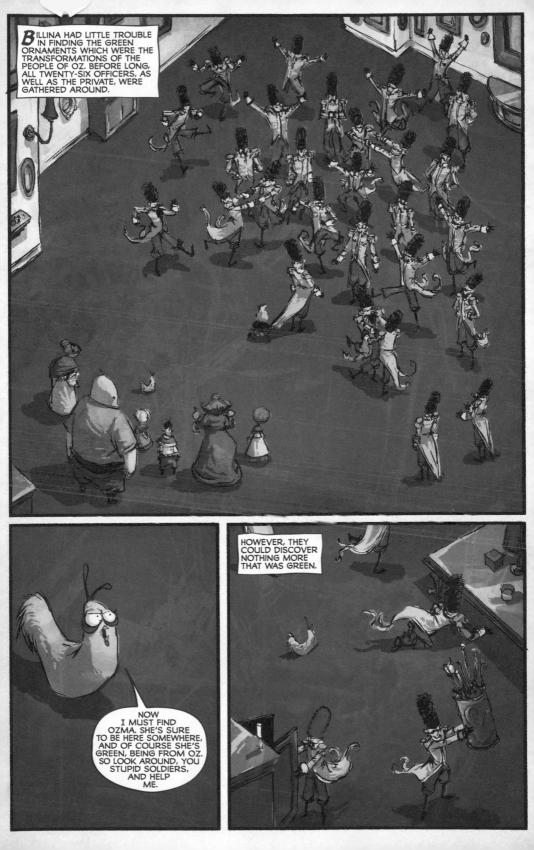

BILLINA HAD LITTLE TROUBLE IN FINDING THE GREEN ORNAMENTS WHICH WERE THE TRANSFORMATIONS OF THE PEOPLE OF OZ. BEFORE LONG, ALL TWENTY-SIX OFFICERS, AS WELL AS THE PRIVATE, WERE GATHERED AROUND.

NOW I MUST FIND OZMA. SHE'S SURE TO BE HERE SOMEWHERE, AND OF COURSE SHE'S GREEN, BEING FROM OZ. SO LOOK AROUND, YOU STUPID SOLDIERS, AND HELP ME.

HOWEVER, THEY COULD DISCOVER NOTHING MORE THAT WAS GREEN.

DOROTHY WENT INTO ANOTHER ROOM.

I COMMAND THE TIN WOODMAN TO RESUME HIS PROPER SHAPE.

SHE REPEATED THIS ATTEMPT THROUGH ALL THE ROOMS OF THE PALACE.

BUT THE TIN WOODMAN DID NOT APPEAR.

I CAN'T IMAGINE WHICH OF THESE THOUSAND OF ORNAMENTS IS OUR TRANSFORMED FRIEND.

I SEE YOU'VE MET WITH FAILURE. YOU DON'T KNOW HOW TO USE MY BELT.

GIVE IT BACK TO ME AND I'LL LET YOU GO FREE--YOU AND ALL THOSE WHO CAME WITH YOU.

AS FOR THE ROYAL FAMILY OF EV, THEY'RE MY SLAVES AND SHALL REMAIN HERE.

THERE'S NO USE PUNISHING THE NOME KING ANY MORE. I'M AFRAID WE'LL HAVE TO GO AWAY WITHOUT OUR FRIEND.

IF HE'S NOT HERE, WE CANNOT RESCUE HIM. POOR NICK CHOPPER! I WONDER WHAT'S BECOME OF HIM.

AND HE OWED ME SIX WEEKS BACK PAY!

Sorrowfully THEY DECIDED TO RETURN TO THE UPPER WORLD WITHOUT THEIR COMPANION.

HEH HEH HEE HEE HEH

LOOK-- THE NOME KING IS STILL ATTEMPTING TO PREVENT OUR ESCAPE!

MAGIC BELT, I COMMAND YOU.

EGGS!

RUN!

AAAH!

A GREAT CROWD GATHERED TO WELCOME THEIR QUEEN AND HER TEN CHILDREN.

I'M *SO* GLAD TO BE RELIEVED OF MY DUTIES TO THE PEOPLE OF EV!

YOU MAY RETAIN YOUR ROOMS AND YOUR CABINET OF HEADS AS LONG AS YOU LIVE.

MY SUBJECTS--HERE IS YOUR FUTURE RULER, KING EVARDO FIFTEENTH! HE'S FIFTEEN YEARS OF AGE, HAS FIFTEEN SILVER BUCKLES ON HIS JACKET, AND IS THE FIFTEENTH EVARDO TO RULE THE LAND OF EV.

THE PEOPLE SHOUTED THEIR APPROVAL FIFTEEN TIMES. EVEN THE WHEELERS PROMISED TO OBEY THE NEW KING.

BILLINA WAS PRESENTED WITH A TOKEN OF ESTEEM.

THEN EVARDO BOWED TO HIS SUBJECTS AND WENT AWAY TO SEE IF HE COULD FIND ANY CAKE IN THE ROYAL PANTRY.

DOROTHY REMEMBERED SOME OF THE PEOPLE WHO HAD BEFRIENDED HER ON HER FIRST VISIT TO OZ.

I DON'T REMEMBER THAT BUILDING. WHAT IS IT?

THAT'S THE ROYAL COLLEGE OF ART AND ATHLETIC PERFECTION. I HAD IT BUILT RECENTLY, AND THE WOGGLE-BUG IS ITS PRESIDENT.

YOU SEE, IN THIS COUNTRY ARE A NUMBER OF YOUTHS WHO DON'T LIKE TO WORK. THE COLLEGE IS AN EXCELLENT PLACE FOR THEM.

WHEN THEY CAME IN SIGHT OF THE EMERALD CITY, THE PEOPLE FLOCKED OUT TO GREET THEIR RULER.

...SO I CONGRATULATE OZMA OF OZ UPON THE SUCCESS OF HER GENEROUS MISSION TO RESCUE THE ROYAL FAMILY OF A NEIGHBORING KINGDOM...

THAT EVENING THERE WAS A GRAND RECEPTION IN THE ROYAL PALACE.

DOROTHY PASSED SEVERAL HAPPY WEEKS AS THE GUEST OF THE ROYAL OZMA.

THEN ONE DAY...

THAT PICTURE--HOW CURIOUS!

YES, THAT'S REALLY A WONDERFUL INVENTION IN MAGIC. IF I WISH TO SEE ANY PART OF THE WORLD OR ANY PERSON LIVING, I NEED ONLY EXPRESS THE WISH AND IT'S SHOWN IN THE PICTURE.

MAY I USE IT?

OF COURSE, MY DEAR.

THEN I'D LIKE TO SEE THE OLD KANSAS FARM AND AUNT EM.

THAT IS A WISE PLAN.

...AND EVERY SATURDAY MORNING YOU'LL LOOK AT ME IN THE MAGIC PICTURE. AND IF YOU SEE ME MAKE THIS SIGNAL--

--I'LL KNOW THAT YOU WANT TO REVISIT THE LAND OF OZ, AND BY MEANS OF THE MAGIC BELT, I'LL WISH THAT YOU MIGHT INSTANTLY RETURN!

AND SO...

HERE'S THE NOME KING'S MAGIC BELT, OZMA.

I want to go to Aus-tral-ia, too, as your ser-vant.

CREE-CREE.

A MACHINE MAN WOULD NEVER DO IN A CIVILIZED COUNTRY. CHANCES ARE THAT YOUR MACHINERY WOULDN'T WORK.

HERE'S TIK-TOK'S KEY. TAKE CARE OF HIM, OZMA.

Variant Cover by Eric Shanower

VARIANT COVER BY ADRIAN ALPHONA